¡MÍRAME, PUEDO CANTAR MÁS!
Look, I Can Sing More!

Lyrics book to accompany
the compact disk and the audio cassette —
with teacher's manual & reproducible student exercises

All songs composed and sung
by Gale Mackey

Pete Butler, rhythm guitar
Safi Madain, percussion and base guitar
Mixed and recorded in Bakersfield and Folsom, California

Book by Gale Mackey with Contee Seely

Command Performance Language Institute
1755 Hopkins Street
Berkeley, CA 94707-2714
Tel/Fax: 510-524-1191
E-mail: consee@aol.com

Lyrics book by Gale Mackey with Contee Seely

Gale Mackey wrote the songs and the great majority of the book. Contee Seely contributed ideas, clarified others, advised, edited, proofread, corrected, and formatted.

Acknowledgments

I would like to thank the following people for their help in the completion of this book and tape: Blaine Ray for providing a pedagogical method over which I overlaid my music teaching strategy. Pete Butler for allowing me to use his recording studio and playing rhythm guitar on the tape. Safi Madain for providing percussion and base guitar. And most of all, my wife Kristen for covering for me by caring for our five children while I banged away at the computer and went off to recording sessions. We also thank Ruth Burton and Lino Nivolo for advice on Spanish.

Gale Mackey can be reached at:
 10105 Sunset Canyon Drive
 Bakersfield, CA 93311
 Phone: 805-665-8135
 E-mail: Cuentista@aol.com

Contee Seely can be reached at the Command Performance Language Institute.

Published by the Command Performance Language Institute, which features Total Physical Response products and other fine products related to language acquisition and language teaching.

To obtain copies of *¡Mírame, puedo cantar!*, contact one of the distributors listed on page 60 or the author (see above) or TPR Storytelling Workshops (contact info on p. *xx*).

First published April, 1997
This printing 2001

Entire contents of this book copyright © 1997 by Gale Mackey and Contee Seely. Permission is hereby granted to reproduce any part of this book for noncommercial classroom or individual use. Rights for all other uses must be obtained from one of the authors.

Entire contents of the cassette entitled *¡Mírame, puedo cantar más!* copyright © 1997 by Gale Mackey.

Entire contents of the CD entitled *¡Mírame, puedo cantar!* y *¡Mírame, puedo cantar más!* copyright © 2001 by Gale Mackey.

Book ISBN 0-929724-30-5
Cassette ISBN 0-929724-29-1
Set—Cassette & Book ISBN 0-929724-31-3
CD ISBN 0-929724-55-0
Set—CD & Book ISBN 0-929724-56-9

CONTENTS

Why Teach Songs	v
How to Teach the Songs	vii
Five Sample Mini-Stories	xvi
Bibliography	xx

TRACK
- CD #2 — El mono y la vaca ... 1
- #7 — Los tres elefantes ... 6
- #9 — Rodolfo ... 12
- #10 — Nacha ... 18
- #11 — El café barato ... 25
- #12 — El restaurante elegante ... 32
- #13 — Los perros olímpicos ... 39
- #14 — El carro de mi familia ... 46
- #15 — Supermujer ... 53

About the Author	60
Distributors	60

HOW TO TEACH THE SONGS

Why Teach Songs

Songs are a known long-term memory device. They encompass three powerful tools — rhythm, rhyme, and melody. They have been used throughout the ages to help people remember things. The ancient troubadours would use music to convey the news and to spread it from village to village. Things of importance always had a song or a rhyme attached to them. With the advent of radio, advertising jingles and songs very quickly became the dominant medium for instilling the memory of products in the minds of listeners. Even today, 40 years since first hearing the jingles, I know that I should "see the U.S.A. in a Chevrolet." And that, as far as Brylcreem is concerned, "a little dab will do you." I also know that "Coca-Cola hits the spot." And that "Nestle makes the very best chaaaawclet." Every denomination of every religion instills in its followers religious principles through the use of songs.

I like to ask people if they have ever studied a language and how it went. Most adults that I have talked to who have had language classes in the past say that they barely remember a thing from their language classes. They usually remember a dialog from the first chapter of the book and, of course, the songs. This informal survey has led me to the conclusion that, if a teacher did nothing but sing songs, she/he would be light-years ahead of the teacher that just taught language through any non-communicative method.

If a song is well learned, it will be well remembered along with its vocabulary. So the trick is to teach songs so that they will be well learned. The keys are *r*epetition, *e*njoyment, and *m*eaningfulness to the learner (REM):

- **R**epetition: The more times that a student can hear a song, the better he/she will learn it — just the way most teenagers remember songs by hearing them over and over and over.

- **E**njoyment: Songs by themselves, if enjoyed by the students, can result in their remembering vocabulary and its usage all their lives. The enjoyment can be of the song itself or the process by which it was learned.

- **M**eaningfulness: If the songs are meaningful or relevant or touch some facet of the students' personal lives, they have a very good chance of absorbing the songs permanently.

I have found that Blaine Ray's TPR Storytelling method, combined with the teaching of songs, is an amazingly powerful tool for instilling vocabulary. Following is a step-by-step approach for teaching vocabulary through the TPR Storytelling method. But first I would like to offer a testimonial about why I use TPR Storytelling almost exclusively in my classroom.

My Testimonial

I left college wanting to be a Spanish teacher. I taught Spanish for several years and realized that I was teaching no more than a couple of kids out of every class, and my colleagues were not doing any better. I wasn't feeling very fulfilled, so I quit teaching Spanish and started a business teaching something I knew how to teach, gymnastics. Ten years later I needed a little extra money, so I accepted a part-time job teaching Spanish. As a benefit of my job, I was sent to a three-day workshop at Oregon State University, where I was exposed to the ideas and writings of James Asher (see Asher, 1996) and Stephen Krashen (see Krashen and Terrell, 1983). From then on my teaching of Spanish was much more successful. I used Contee Seely's book *¡Español con impacto!* (1992) and was having success! I taught 35 classes, each once a week, and my students were learning more than my previous students had learned when I taught them every day of the week. I was excited that I was using my college major in my work and teaching the language of my heart.

Then in April of 1992 I attended a CLTA (California Language Teachers Association) workshop given by Blaine Ray. He had brought two of his Spanish I students with him as demonstrators. These ninth-graders, who had had a total of seven months of Spanish, were amazingly conversant in Spanish. Contee Seely writes about this workshop in Chapter 4 of *TPR Is More Than Commands — At All Levels* (1995: 39-40). I returned to my classroom and used Blaine Ray's method as best I could. I can easily say that my students learned twice as much in half the time! Since then I applied for and got a job at the school where Blaine Ray works, Stockdale High School in Bakersfield, California. Stockdale High has been Blaine Ray's language teaching laboratory for the past six years. He has been very fortunate to be working together with conscientious teachers who wanted to be as successful as possible. When they saw the difference between the results they were getting and the results he was getting in language acquisition, they converted to Blaine's method. I have learned that the closer I stick to the method Blaine Ray invented, the more my students succeed in developing spoken fluency and the more they progress in all aspects of Spanish.

The TPR Storytelling Method and How It Works
(or How to Teach Songs with TPR Storytelling)

First, let me say that the tried-and-true method of having the students just read the songs while singing them is effective and produces long-term memory. So often it is the case, however, when teaching songs, that the students learn the songs but have no idea what half the words mean, and the half that they do know they can't use outside of the context of the song. Not so with the method I am about to share with you. It is much faster and more effective. The students end up knowing the vocabulary so well that they can put it to use in their own sentences.

Note that the classes referred to below are high school classes that meet 50 minutes each day Monday through Friday.

Teaching the Vocabulary

The TPR Storytelling method of teaching songs begins with the teaching of the new vocabulary of the song. The vocabulary is taught through the use of gestures (or "hand TPR") and mini-stories; this is where both TPR and storytelling are involved in the process of learning songs.

1. Three words are presented, one at time. The meaning of each word is given as it is presented.

2. The teacher then goes over these words attaching an appropriate gesture to each one.

3. The students imitate the gestures. Each time the teacher says one of the words, the students make the corresponding gesture along with the teacher. The teacher varies the order in which she/he says the words.

4. The teacher then delays his/her gesture after saying each word to see if the students are making the gestures on their own with only the words of the target language as their stimulus.

5. The teacher uses mnemonic devices, or associations, whenever possible. Blaine Ray has done several informal studies on the benefit of associations as ways of remembering a word or concept. He has found that there are certain mnemonic

devices that elicit almost 100 per cent retention of the target words by the students. Some examples of these are: "*Are you the* help?" for *ayuda* (help), "Walk *on the* floor" for *anda* (walk), and "*You're a* baby" for *llora* (cry). In each instance the English sentence contains sounds similar to those of the Spanish word, and the meaning of the word (or a related concept) is included in the sentence.

6. If at all possible, the teacher asks personalized questions and/or says novel statements or commands to the students relating to the target vocabulary, providing several examples per word. Let's say the word is *cage*. He/she could ask: "What is a cage? Who has a cage at home? What room is your cage in? Do you have a cage? What is in your cage? Where can you find cages here in (name of your city or town)? What is the difference between a cage and a house?" (If a question can be personalized to a student, by all means this should be done.)

    Or he/she could issue the following commands: "Pretend that you are in a cage. Pretend that you are a monkey in a cage." Or: "Make a tiny cage. Take your nose off and put it in the tiny cage. Put food in the cage for your nose. Open the door to the cage and scratch the nose in the cage." It is not always possible to make novel commands, statements, or personalized questions; however, when it *is* possible, your class will jump ahead by leaps and bounds. In Spanish I in high school, the teacher does most of the talking, using simple questions which can be answered with just one or two words. (See numbers 1 and 2 on p. *xi* for more on questions that students can give short answers to.) Towards the end of Spanish I, the students in the class usually contribute more to the conversation with simple sentences, and at the Spanish II level students can produce more involved sentences. They usually won't answer with full sentences, unless they are asked to.

7. Personalized mini-mini-stories: put the word you are practicing in a student-centered mini-mini-story. The more bizarre, exaggerated, or surprising the mini-mini-stories are, the more effective they are. For example:

    > John goes to the zoo to see the monkey. The monkey thinks that John is very interesting. He makes some popcorn and sits in the cage and watches John.

It is not usually possible to tell a mini-mini-story for each word on the vocabulary list, but whenever it can be done, there is very high retention of the target words.

8. When the teacher believes that the students understand all three words whenever they hear them, he/she introduces three more words, going through the same process with each group of three words (and checking after each set of three have been worked on to be sure the whole class understands all the words presented up to that point) — until he/she has taught three or four groups of three words.

9. Then he/she has them do the actions (gestures) with their eyes closed while he/she says *all* the words again. If some students open their eyes or if they don't know the actions for certain words, the teacher marks these words on a word list and re-teaches those words. The teacher should always have a list that she/he is working from to keep track of which words have been well learned and which words need to be re-taught.

10. The Barometer: To make sure the class knows all the words well, the teacher picks out a student that she/he knows to be in the lowest third of the class and quizzes that student on the words orally. If he/she misses some words, these words are taught all over again using all of the above procedures. The idea is that if this student knows the words, then *everybody* knows them.

Mini-Stories

When the teacher is satisfied that all the words have been internalized, she/he tells a "mini-story" (a short story 8 to 15 sentences long) which she/he has made up before class, using the learned vocabulary. Sometimes she/he tells a "mini-mini-story" (3 to 7 sentences). The stories should be highly relevant to the students' lives. For example, for teenagers, there should be many stories that include driving, dating, dances, school, sports, etc. Five to eight mini-stories are used for each song. If mini-mini-stories are used, there might be more than eight. (The main advantages of using the *mini-mini*-stories are that students learn them quicker and better (as evidenced by the reaction time of the students during comprehension checks). On the other hand, the advantage of the longer *mini*-stories is that they can be developed a bit more and so are generally more entertaining and pertinent to the lives of students.) Mini-mini-stories can be: (1) each a separate story, (2) each one half of a mini-story, or (3) a separate story that makes use of half of the vocabulary that's in a mini-story (in the latter two cases the mini-story is done immediately afterwards). In any event, the stories should be zany and preposterous and, altogether, they should include all of the vocabulary items from the song which are new to the class. On pages *xvii* to *xix* below is a full set of examples of five mini-stories based on the vocabulary of the first song, "El mono y la vaca." The stories are dealt with one by one.

WARNING: If you try to accomplish the story phase of the process with culturally relevant stories from a textbook or reader, you will lose the interest of the class; most students will "check out" mentally. They usually couldn't care less what Paco and Isabel are doing in South America. They want to know what their classmates are doing and how they are doing it. Also, if you read the story to the class instead of telling it by looking at the guide words yourself, you will lose the class. Keep the words in mind or glance at them as you tell the story, but DO NOT READ THE STORY.

Acting Out the Stories and the Involvement Hypothesis

A previously selected group of students in the class acts out the stories while the teacher is telling them. This is when the class clowns come in handy and can really spice up a class. This experience seems to be what gels the vocabulary for everyone involved. The experience and its related vocabulary relevant to the students' immediate lives will remain with the students.

I have no scientific evidence for the following statement; however, experience in the classroom has shown me that it is true. I believe strongly that the degree of entertainment or involvement of the students with the input (in this case, the mini-stories) is directly related to how well students acquire a new language. A corollary to this hypothesis is that if the students find the material irrelevant, foreign, and consequently not entertaining, total acquisition shutdown occurs. Once this happens, it takes lots of effort on the part of the teacher to help the students get back on track and be accepting of the new vocabulary. The students must feel an emotional need to know. What many people don't realize is that most vocabulary in the first language is acquired through emotional involvement with parents and family. We need to try to artificially re-create this environment in the classroom so that the students feel an emotional need to know what is being said.

Learning to Tell the Mini-stories through Aural Comprehension Exercises

Next, the teacher does several aural comprehension exercises with the class. These exercises accomplish the following purposes: (1) they check the students' comprehension of the mini-story (for teacher and students), challenging the students to see what they understand — they do pay attention because they want to get it; (2) they serve as further comprehensible input, allowing the students to become more familiar with the story; and (3) most of them help students to start telling the story, since most of the student responses are words, phrases, or full sentences in the story. In other words they help students to learn to tell the story. They are very helpful in developing students' ability to produce their own utterances. As with most other production activities in TPR Storytelling, we are not looking for perfect grammar and pronunciation but rather for reasonably quick and clear expression of meaning.

1. The teacher asks low-level questions that require one- or two-word answers. There are two types: (a) yes-or-no questions, e.g., "¿Rodolfo tiene mucha suerte?" (Is Rodolfo very lucky?) and (b) question-word questions with *qué, quién(es), a quién(es), dónde, adónde, cuándo, cuál(es), cuánto(s), cómo y de qué manera* (what, who, whom, where, when, which, how much, how many, how, in what way).

2. He/she asks slightly higher-level questions or "either/or" questions that require choosing between two options, e.g., "Rodolfo juega golf o va a un restaurante con Julia Roberts?" (Does Rodolfo play golf or go to a restaurant with Julia Roberts?) or "¿Adónde viaja Rodolfo, a Brooklyn o a París?" (Where does Rodolfo travel to, Brooklyn or Paris?) Notice that the above question words can be used in either/or questions.

3. The teacher tells the story, pausing frequently for the students to fill in the pauses by shouting out the appropriate missing words, e.g., "El avión de Rodolfo _____ en el oceanito y un _____ lo rescata." (Rodolfo's airplane _____ into the ocean and a _____ rescues him.)

4. The teacher tells the story and makes mistakes that the students are to correct, e.g., "Rodolfo va a París en tren" (Rodolfo goes to Paris by train.) — in which case we are looking for a student response of "¡No, no, no! ¡Rodolfo va a París en avión!" (No, no, no! Rodolfo goes to Paris by plane!) or just "¡No, no! ¡En avión!"

5. The teacher asks open questions, e.g., "¿Por qué le gusta a Rodolfo viajar tanto?" (Why does Rodolfo like to travel so much?) The open questions are asked if it seems that the other levels of questioning were easy for the students. They are often *why* questions.

Sometimes some of the students have trouble answering some questions. Usually if they can't answer the questions, it is not because they are not understanding; it is because they can't yet easily make the switch from understood language to produced language. I have found that if I just let them say the answers in English, they can usually say the answers in Spanish right afterwards.

Guide Words
(Developed by Joe Neilson of Salpointe Catholic High School in Phoenix, Arizona)

The teacher has the list of words that the students have been working on written on the board (*without* translations), and the students work in pairs taking turns using the words and phrases (written in the same sequence as they appear in the mini-story) as guides in telling the story to each other. Then some students are picked to tell the story to the class. This helps them acquire good spelling and correct grammar. If the process of teaching the vocabulary was thorough enough, all, or almost all, of the students should be able to retell the story.

Guide Pictures

Next, ideally, a series of pictures depicting the chain of events in the story can be made available to the students in some form. Otherwise, the students can draw their own sequential pictures depicting the story. Then they tell the story, referring to the pictures as memory guides. The second-year book *¡Mírame, puedo hablar más!* by Blaine Ray and Joe Neilson (1992) has quite few of such mini-stories in pictures. (Most of the songs on *¡Mírame, puedo cantar!* are based on the longer stories in this book.) Since there are no ready-made pictures in print for the mini-stories based on vocabulary in the songs and because it is so time-consuming to have the kids draw them, I usually skip this step but include it occasionally for variety.

Every day, before the inputting of new vocabulary, there should be a review of the old vocabulary (after the students have learned to tell the first mini-story based on the vocabulary of a song). This is done by having students quickly take turns in telling the old mini-stories.

The process of working with a mini-story generally takes about two 50-minute classes. The story is acted out by two or three different groups of actors, who always put a different spin on the original rendition, making it that much more entertaining. Another thing that adds flavor is changing the story by adding more preposterous and/or ridiculous situations. The teacher has the students, in pairs, make up new stories with the same vocabulary and picks a few of the more interesting stories to be acted out for the whole class. The idea is to use the same vocabulary in all the different stories that are acted out — repetition without boredom and *with* creativity.

After about two days of this (maybe three if there are still more than a few students that do not fully understand and cannot retell the stories), the teacher begins again, doing all the above steps with the next list of 10 to 20 words and another mini-story and so on. Sometimes this process goes slowly. On the other hand, sometimes after only one day the vocabulary is completely assimilated and anyone that is called on can retell the story. The teacher should not be afraid to go through the storytelling phase as many times as are necessary for full assimilation.

WARNING: If after having gone through the whole process the teacher finds that many students are not understanding very much, she/he needs to start the whole process over with the same vocabulary. This happens when teachers fool themselves into thinking that the students "have it" when they don't — wishful thinking. It is easy to believe that all the students understand when the students give choral responses to questions about the stories. Teachers should be wary of this, because just ten students responding correctly in a class of 30 or 40 can sound as if the whole class has full comprehension. It is best for the teacher to ask various middle- and lower-middle-ability students to give oral translations of words and/or to retell the story. If they know the vocabulary and the story, you can bet that the great majority of the class knows them also.

The books *Mini-Stories for ¡Mírame, puedo hablar!* by Joe Neilson and Blaine Ray (1996) and *Mini-Stories for Look, I Can Talk!* (with the mini-stories in English) by Blaine Ray and Joe Neilson (1996) contain a lot more mini-stories and give more information on how to use them in the classroom.

This is not all there is to the TPR Storytelling method (see Ray and Seely, 1997); however, it is the main and most important part and is all you need to teach songs effectively.

Song Presentation

1. As you present a song to a class, tell the students that they are not allowed to sing. Play the songs and have them do the actions for the words in the song as the song is playing. Some songs are very fast and it is difficult to keep up with the actions, so you can have them make sure that they at least do one action per line in such songs. Practice the song in this manner three to five days in a row.

Usually after a while you will hear a few kids begin to sing the song even though you have told them not to sing. This is your cue to let them start to sing.

2. Put the song on the overhead projector and have them sing. Tell them that they don't have to do the actions any more. They will be relieved and will usually sing. Sing in this manner five to seven times over two or three days.

3. While they are singing, play the song on the stereo or cassette player, and every few lines turn the volume down all the way so that the students are singing unassisted by the words and music.

4. Take away the overhead and see if they have it by memory. You might do the actions yourself to help them remember. Then again periodically turn off the volume of the stereo for longer and longer times until they seem to "have it" without even needing the stereo. By this time the vocabulary is fully locked in. Even if some of the students still don't sing, you can bet they know the words if they have been active participants otherwise.

5. At this point you can go to another song and start the process all over again, or you can play the music only (on Side B on the cassette) and have the students sing with the music. This is not necessary but it is a nice touch to give everybody a feeling of closure and accomplishment. WARNING: do not do this activity more than 20 minutes per day, especially with high school or younger students. Activities should change every 15 to 20 minutes, or you will start to have trouble on your hands.

As the students gain mastery of more and more songs, it is fun once or twice a week to start class by having them sing their entire repertoire either by rote or with the help of the audio or with both audio and visual cues, depending on how well they know the songs. Have fun!

An important note: As Professor Stephen Krashen is so fond of telling us, language is learned by input, not by output, so if you end up with a bunch of non-singers, remember that as long as they do the actions to the song, showing you that they are understanding, they don't really need to sing a note in order to be learning. It may not be what you wanted, but the fact is that if they listen to a song and can show understanding of it through gestures (actions), they are learning more than students who are just reading it and singing it.

Following is a list of words and stories that can be used to input the vocabulary in context for the song "El mono y la vaca." After the words have been fully inputted with actions, novel statements, and questions and answers, the students act out these stories. Do one of these stories every two days (i.e., 50-minute class periods). Make sure each mini-story is acted out at least twice.

By the way, if you are already a TPR Storytelling teacher using the ¡Mírame, puedo hablar! series by Blaine Ray and Joe Neilson, you will only need to teach a little bit of vocabulary, because the stories in this series already include most of the words that are in the songs and of course many more. The first two songs are based on Chapters 2 and 7 in ¡Mírame, puedo hablar!, the first-year book. The other seven songs are based on Chapters 1 through 6 in ¡Mírame, puedo hablar más!

If you have already gone through Blaine Ray's first three lists and are now working on the list for Chapter 2 of ¡Mírame, puedo hablar! ("La vaca y el mono"), there are only a few words left to teach in order to prepare your students to learn the song "El mono y la vaca." You just need to make up a simple mini-story with the few words that are in the song but are not in Chapter 2 and then go through the procedure outlined above for teaching mini-stories (pp. *ix-xiii*). You can teach the song instead of the main story in the text. Or, if you really want to sink the vocabulary into your students' brains, you can teach both, a song and a story. You can do either one first; it makes no difference. Either way, the second of the two can be taught quickly and easily.

Words set to rhythm, rhyme, and melody are for most students relatively easy to commit to memory and to retrieve. Part of the reason for this seems to be emotional involvement on the part of students (gestures, tapping toes, singing, and smiling that often occur along with songs are overt indications of emotional involvement), which occurs with songs to a greater degree than with most language-learning material. When a student is speaking and wants to form sentences, she/he can pull up from memory a model phrase or sentence (with a needed word, form, or pattern) from a song which can serve as a monitor in case of doubt. It is an easier and more pleasant monitor to install and use than the grammar rule-type monitor described by Krashen, though it is still not instantaneous. In the longer run, the repeated process of learning stories and manipulating their content develops in students a "feeling for correctness" (as Blaine Ray calls it), which is a sign that a grammatical aspect of the target language has been acquired by the student. This is a step beyond any other type of monitor and is what we aim for and usually achieve with the TPR Storytelling method.

For teachers who have not been using the ¡Mírame, puedo hablar! series, I have included here five mini-stories which are based on the vocabulary of the first song on the tape. Before each mini-story you will find a vocabulary list which includes a few extra words for the particular story. The mini-stories, when acted out, and the songs, when learned and gestured, are the most powerful part of this teaching procedure. It is in the songs and the mini-stories that students have an opportunity to express themselves in Spanish. In learning to tell mini-stories and in actually telling them, they develop spoken fluency. In the songs, when they learn them through the TPR Storytelling procedures, they demonstrate a thorough knowledge of the material, so thorough that the more they use these procedures the more they can put this material to use freely in fluent oral speech. Happily, this method allows many opportunities for students to have fun. If your students are having fun, much of your work is done.

Student Rapport

An essential aspect of TPR Storytelling is student rapport. For it to work well, it is imperative that there is a degree of mutual caring between the teacher and the students. Not that teachers don't usually care for their students. Quite the contrary, almost all teachers care for their students; that's one reason they are teachers. However, not all teachers know *how* to care for their students. Here are some ideas that have helped me, ideas that I have learned from observing Blaine Ray, who I consider a master at the art of achieving good rapport in the classroom. I'm sure most of these items would relate to any age group and/or cultural mix.

1. Find out as much as you can about your students. In high school, look in yearbooks and student newspapers for gems about your students and what they have accomplished or are accomplishing in sports, drama, service club activities, etc. Have them write you a note in English for extra credit, telling you anything they wish to share about their lives.
2. Mention the names of your students in the mini-stories that you tell and highlight their talents and interests.
3. Shake each student's hand as he/she walks into your class.
4. Take time to listen to your students on an individual basis at least a few minutes each class period or between class periods.
5. Set up the class rules so that no one is allowed to make fun of or verbally abuse anybody else.
6. Bring up students' names often while you are teaching.
7. Don't miss a chance to notice creative changes in apparel and or appearance.
8. See the positive side of every situation.
9. Avoid and prevent adversarial comments and relationships with and between students.
10. Let students know that you appreciate them.

♪♪¡Mírame, puedo cantar más!♪♪

Vocabulary and Five Sample Mini-Stories for the Song "El mono y la vaca"

Cuentito 1

duerme	is sleeping
ronca	is snoring
fuerte	loud
está muy enojado	is very angry
coge	grabs
vaso	glass
agua (femenino)	water
lo tira	throws it
se despierta	wakes up him/herself
hace mucho calor	it's very hot

Pedro duerme en la clase y ronca muy fuerte. El maestro está muy enojado. Coge un vaso de agua y lo tira en la cabeza de Pedro. Pedro se despierta y dice: "Gracias, hace mucho calor".

Cuentito 2

zoológico	zoo
mono	monkey
muy pobre	very poor
tiene hambre	is hungry
los cacahuates	the peanuts
grita	yells
¡ay caramba!	oh darn!, my gosh!
dice	says
ven acá	come here
jaula	cage
come	eat
por	through
barras	bars
vive	lives
con	with
flaco	thin, slender

♪♪¡Mírame, puedo cantar más!♪♪

Pancho va al zoológico. Él es muy pobre y tiene hambre. Él mira a un mono en una jaula. El mono come muchos cacahuates. Pancho grita: "¡Ay caramba!" porque hay muchos cacahuates. El mono dice: "Ven acá. Come mis cacahuates." Pancho entra en la jaula del mono por las barras porque él es muy flaco. Pancho vive con el mono y ahora está muy feliz y no tiene hambre.

Cuentito 3

ve que	sees that
vaca	cow
muy fuerte	very strong
tira	throws
China	China
entonces	then
por favor	please
no tengo	I don't have
así que	so
la tira	throws her

Un muchacho camina en la calle y ve que una muchacha está debajo de una vaca. El muchacho es muy fuerte y levanta la vaca y tira la vaca a China. La muchacha dice: "Muchas gracias." El muchacho dice: "Cinco dólares por favor." La muchacha dice: "No tengo dinero." Así que el muchacho agarra a la muchacha y la tira a China.

Cuentito 4

rico	rich
superrico	super rich
guapo	handsome
pantalones	pants
bonitos	pretty
corbata	tie
zapatos	shoes
casa	house
grande	big
triste	sad
necesita	needs
está llorando	is crying
sale	goes out, leaves
pobres	poor
viven	live

la calle	the street
invita	invites
dicen	say
hacen una fiesta	have a party

Hay un mono que es superrico. Él es muy guapo. Tiene pantalones bonitos y una corbata y unos zapatos Nike y vive en una casa muy grande. Hay un problema: el mono está muy triste. Necesita otros monos. El mono rico está llorando. Él sale de su casa y mira a muchos monos pobres que viven en la calle. Él invita a los monos a su casa. Los monos dicen: "Gracias" y entran en la casa del mono rico y hacen una fiesta. El mono rico está muy feliz.

Cuentito 5

va comprando	goes around shopping for
por fin	at last
encuentra	finds
lo compra	buys it
le da	gives her
las llaves	the keys
para ti	for you
tienes	you have
propio	own
agarra	grabs
piso	floor
para mí	for me
quiero	I want

Papá va comprando un carro para Matilde. Por fin él encuentra un Mercedes-Benz y lo compra para Matilde. Él le da las llaves a Matilde y dice: "Para ti, Matilde. Tú tienes tu propio carro." Matilde agarra las llaves y tira las llaves en el piso y dice: "¡No es para mí! ¡Yo quiero un Toyota!"

BIBLIOGRAPHY

Asher, James J. 1996. *Learning Another Language Through Actions: The Complete Teacher's Guidebook*, 5th ed. Los Gatos, CA: Sky Oaks.

Krashen, Stephen D. and Tracy D. Terrell. 1983. *The Natural Approach*. Hayward, CA: Alemany Press. Currently available from Tappan, NJ: Prentice-Hall.

Neilson, Joe and Blaine Ray. 1996. *Mini-Stories for **Look, I Can Talk!*** Bakersfield, CA: TPR Storytelling Workshops. (available in English and Spanish; expected in French in 1997)

Ray, Blaine. 1996. *Mini-Stories for **Look, I'm Still Talking!*** Bakersfield, CA: TPR Storytelling Workshops. (currently available only in English; English version can be adapted for Spanish and French)

Ray, Blaine and Joe Neilson. 1996. *Mini-Stories for **Look, I Can Talk More!*** Bakersfield, CA: TPR Storytelling Workshops. (currently available only in English; English version can be adapted for Spanish and French)

Ray, Blaine, Joe Neilson, Dave Cline and Carole Stevens. 1992. *Look, I Can Talk More!* Los Gatos, CA: Sky Oaks. (available in English, Spanish, French)

Ray, Blaine. 1990. *Look, I Can Talk!* Los Gatos, CA: Sky Oaks. (available in English, Spanish, French, German)

Seely, Contee. 1992. *¡Español con impacto!*, 6th ed. Berkeley, CA: Command Performance Language Institute. (temporarily out of print; the 7th edition is in preparation)

ADDITIONAL WORKS OF INTEREST (revised, 2001)

McKay, Todd. 2000. *TPR Storytelling, Especially for Children in Elementary and Middle School*. Student books, transparencies, testing packets (years 1, 2 and 3; available in Spanish, French and English) and teacher's guidebook (with James J. Asher). Los Gatos, CA: Sky Oaks.

Ray, Blaine. 1992. *Look, I Can Talk! Teacher's Guidebook*, 2nd ed. (for Spanish, French, German, and English) Los Gatos, CA: Sky Oaks.

Ray, Blaine. 1993. *Teaching Grammar Communicatively*. New York and Roanoke, VA: Gessler Publishing.

Ray, Blaine. 1995. *TPR Storytelling Video*. Bakersfield, CA: TPR Storytelling Workshops and Berkeley, CA: Command Performance.

Ray, Blaine and Joe Neilson. *Look, I'm Still Talking!* 1993. Berkeley, CA: Command Performance. (available in English, Spanish, and French)

Ray, Blaine and Contee Seely. 1998. *Fluency Through TPR Storytelling*, 2nd ed. Berkeley, CA: Command Performance.

Seely, Contee and Elizabeth Kuizenga Romijn. 1998. *TPR Is More Than Commands—At All Levels*, 2nd ed. Berkeley, CA: Command Performance.

All works by Blaine Ray are available from:

> Blaine Ray Workshops
> 3820 Amur Maple Drive
> Bakersfield, CA 93311
> Phone: 888-373-1920 (toll free) or 661-665-9523
> Fax: 661-665-8071
> E-mail: BlaineRay@aol.com

Several other good TPR Storytelling materials are also available from:

For elementary and middle schools:
> C.W. Publishing
> P.O. Box 9064
> Scottsdale, AZ 85252
> (800) TPR IS FUN = (800) 877-4738
> Fax: (602) 963-3463
> TPRISFUN@aol.com
> www.tprstorytelling.com

For secondary schools:
> Melinda Forward
> 11555 Highway 377 South
> Fort Worth, TX 76126
> (817) 249-8653
> mforward@eaze.net

See also the list of **distributors** on page 60, the final page of this book.

Vocabulario para "El mono y la vaca"

mono	monkey
se duerme	falls asleep
ronca	snore
despierta a	wakes up (someone else)
vaca	cow
se despierta	wakes up him/herself
coge	she grabs
vaso	glass
lo tira	throws it
cara	face
grita	yells
soy	I am
pobre	poor
¡ay caramba!	oh darn!, my gosh!
tengo	I have
los pantalones	the pants
zapatos	shoes
ni	nor
sale	leaves
llorando	crying
entonces	then
va comprando	goes around shopping for
para ti	for you
para mí	for me
tienes	you have

♪♪¡Mírame, puedo cantar más!♪♪

El mono y la vaca

El mono se duerme. (ronca ronca)
Se duerme en la calle. (ronca ronca)
Despierta a la vaca. (ronca ronca)
Se despierta enojada. (ronca ronca)
Coge un vaso de agua.
Lo tira en la cara.

El mono grita: (ronca ronca)
"¡Soy mono pobre! (¡ay caramba!)
No tengo una casa. (¡ay caramba!)
No tengo pantalones, (¡ay caramba!)
zapatos ni corbata."

La vaca sale llorando.
Entonces va comprando
una casa. (¡ay caramba!)
"¡Para ti! ¡Para ti! Mono, ¡para ti!"
"¡Para mí! ¡Para mí! Vaca, ¡para mí!"
"¡Sí! ¡Sí! ¡Sí! ¡Sí! ¡Tienes tu propia casa!"

The song "El mono y la vaca" is based on the story "La vaca y el mono" in Chapter 2 of ¡Mírame, puedo hablar! by Blaine Ray.

♪♪ ¡Mírame, puedo cantar más! ♪♪

Ejercicio nº 1

El mono _____ _____ . (ronca _____)

Se duerme en la _____ . (ronca ronca)

_____ a la vaca.

Se despierta _____ . (ronca ronca)

_____ un vaso de agua.

Lo _____ en la cara.

El _____ grita. (ronca ronca)

"¡Soy mono _____ ! (¡ay _____ !)

_____ _____ una casa. (¡ay caramba!)

No tengo _____ , (¡ay caramba!)

zapatos ni _____ ."

La vaca sale _____ .

_____ va comprando

_____ casa. (¡ay caramba!)

"¡Para ti! ¡ _____ _____ ! Mono, ¡para ti!"

"¡Para mí! ¡ _____ _____ ! Vaca, ¡para mí!"

"¡Sí! ¡Sí! ¡Sí! ¡Sí! ¡Tienes tu _____ casa!"

♪♪¡Mírame, puedo cantar más!♪♪

Ejercicio nº 2

Haz un círculo alrededor de la *c* o la *f*.   cierto   falso

  1. El mono duerme en una casa.   c   f

  2. La vaca duerme en una casa.   c   f

  3. El mono está enojado porque la vaca ronca.   c   f

  4. El mono grita: "¡Soy mono rico!"   c   f

  5. La vaca recoge un vaso de leche.   c   f

  6. La vaca llora porque el mono pega a la vaca.   c   f

  7. El mono tira la vaca a la calle.   c   f

  8. La vaca coge los pantalones del mono.   c   f

  9. La vaca sale llorando porque el mono no tiene casa.   c   f

10. La vaca dice: "Tienes tu propia casa."   c   f

Ejercicio nº 3

One-word answers are OK in this exercise.

11. ¿El mono duerme en la calle o en la casa? _____

12. ¿La vaca se ríe o está enojada cuando se despierta? _____

13. ¿La vaca recoge un vaso de agua o de Coca-Cola? _____

14. ¿Lo tira en la cara o en la pierna? _____

15. ¿El mono canta o grita? _____

16. ¿El mono grita: "¡Soy mono pobre!" o ¡Soy mono alto!"? _____

17. ¿El mono grita: "¡No tengo pantalones!" o "¡No tengo orejas!"? _____

18. ¿La vaca va comprando una taza o una casa? _____

19. ¿La vaca compra una casa para el mono o para el caballo? _____

20. ¿El mono y la vaca dicen: "Sí, sí, sí, sí" o "No, no, no, no"? _____

Ejercicio nº 4

Dibuja el cuento del mono y la vaca en estos seis rectángulos. Entonces cuéntale el cuento a tu pareja.

1	2
3	4
5	6

♪♪ *¡Mírame, puedo cantar más!* ♪♪

Vocabulario para "Los tres elefantes"

el elefante	the elephant
prueba	tastes
sopa	soup
ni	not even
caliente	hot
paciente	patient
grita	yells
me gusta	it pleases me (I like it)
aburrido	bored
por	through
medio	middle
el bosque	the forest
me voy	I'm going
después	later
cansado	tired
estoy	I am
vuelvo	I return
pa'	in order to (slang for *para*)
rompe	breaks
mientras	while
las flores	the flowers
brillan	shine
come	eats
bebe	drinks
Coca	Coca-Cola
se sube	climbs up
recámara	bedroom
se mete	gets into
sin	without
comodita (cómoda)	comfortable
regresan	return
el comedor	the dining room
buscan	look for
gota	drop
¡Qué horror!	how horrible
dormitorio	bedroom
despierta	wakes up
asustada	scared

Los tres elefantes

El grande elefante prueba la sopa y ahora enojado está.
Está muy caliente y no es muy paciente y grita: "¡No me gusta!"

Estribillo:
Aburrido en la casa estoy. Por el medio del bosque me voy.
Y después cuando cansado estoy, vuelvo pa' comer mi comida.

Una muchacha entra en la casa y rompe una silla
mientras caminan los tres elefantes por donde las flores brillan.

Estribillo

Come la sopa y bebe una Coca. Se sube a la recámara.
Se mete en la cama sin las pijamas y ahora comodita está.

Estribillo

Los tres elefantes regresan a casa y entran en el comedor.
Buscan la sopa. No hay ni una gota y gritan: "¡Qué horror! ¡Qué horror!"

Estribillo

Los tres elefantes se suben pa' arriba y en el dormitorio entran.
La chica despierta asustada y alerta salta por la ventana.

Estribillo

> The song "Los tres elefantes" is based on the story of the same name in Chapter 7 of *¡Mírame, puedo hablar!* by Blaine Ray.

♪♪ ¡Mírame, puedo cantar más! ♪♪

Ejercicio nº 1

El grande elefante _____ la sopa y ahora enojado está.

Está muy _____ y no es muy paciente y _____ : "¡No me gusta!"

Estribillo:

¡ _____ en la casa estoy! Por el _____ del bosque me voy.

Y después _____ cansado estoy, _____ pa' comer mi comida.

Una muchacha entra en la casa y _____ una silla

_____ caminan los tres elefantes por donde las flores _____ .

Estribillo:

Aburrido en la casa _____ . Por el medio del _____ me voy.

Y _____ cuando cansado estoy, vuelvo pa' _____ mi _____ .

Come la _____ y bebe una Coca. Se sube a la _____ .

____ _____ en la cama, sin las pijamas y ahora _____ está.

Estribillo

Los tres elefantes _____ a casa y entran en el comedor.

_____ la sopa. No hay ni una _____ y gritan: "¡Qué horror! ¡Qué horror!"

Estribillo

Los tres elefantes ____ _____ pa' arriba y en el dormitorio entran.

La chica _____ asustada y alerta salta por la ventana.

8

Estribillo
Ejercicio nº 2

Haz un círculo alrededor de la *c* o la *f*.　　　　　　　　　　cierto　falso

1. El elefante pequeño prueba la sopa y está enojado.　　　c　　f
2. La muchacha grita: "¡No me gusta!"　　　　　　　　　　c　　f
3. El elefante grande dice que está aburrido.　　　　　　　c　　f
4. La muchacha entra en la casa y rompe una mesa.　　　　c　　f
5. Los elefantes caminan en el bosque.　　　　　　　　　　c　　f
6. La muchacha bebe una Coca.　　　　　　　　　　　　　c　　f
7. La muchacha lleva pijamas en la cama.　　　　　　　　c　　f
8. La muchacha no está cómoda.　　　　　　　　　　　　c　　f
9. Los tres elefantes no regresan a la casa.　　　　　　　　c　　f
10. En la mesa no hay ni una gota de sopa.　　　　　　　　c　　f

Ejercicio nº 3

Responde con frases completas.

11. ¿La muchacha entra en la casa o sale de la casa?

___

12. ¿El elefante grande está enojado porque la sopa está caliente o fría?

___

13. ¿Una muchacha rompe una silla o rompe una cama?

___

14. ¿La muchacha bebe un vodka o bebe una Coca?

___

15. Cuando los elefantes entran en el comedor, ¿buscan sopa o cacahuates?

___

♪♪¡Mírame, puedo cantar más!♪♪

Ejercicio nº 4

16. ¿Por qué gritan: "¡Qué horror! ¡Qué horror!"
    _____

17. ¿Qué hacen los tres elefantes cuando se suben al segundo piso?
    _____

18. ¿Por qué salta la chica por la ventana?
    _____

19. ¿Por qué no lleva pijamas la chica?
    _____

20. ¿Por qué no es muy paciente el elefante grande?
    _____

Ejercicio nº 5

Haz seis dibujos que representan el cuento de los tres elefantes y cuéntaselo a tu compañero(a) de clase.

1	2
3	4
5	6

♪♪¡Mírame, puedo cantar más!♪♪

Vocabulario para "Rodolfo"

el hombre	the man
juega	plays
el chicle	the chewing gum
chiclitos	gum (a cute word for chewing gum)
mil	one thousand
cada	each
hoyo	hole
hoyito	little hole
su juego	his game
tiene dinero	has money
conoce	is acquainted with
todo le va bien	everything goes well for him
siempre	always
muy bien	very well
¡Qué casualidad!	What a coincidence!
entonces	then
la invita	invites her
lo acepta	accepts it (the offer)
no quiere ofender	does not want to offend
aventurero	adventurer
crucero	cruise ship
la suerte	luck
siempre	always
le va muy bien	goes well for him
paga	pays
también	also
le da	gives him
beso	kiss
se sube a	gets into (a vehicle)
nuestro	our
el avión	the airplane
océano	ocean
oceanito	little ocean
muertos	dead
le regalan	they give him a gift of (they "gift" him)
tres millones	three million
las habitaciones	the dwellings

Rodolfo

Rodolfo es un hombre que juega golf muy bien.
Juega con Arnold Palmer, Jack Nicklaus también.
No juega por chiclitos, tampoco centavitos.
Juega por mil dólares por cada hoyito.

Estribillo nº 1:
Rodolfo.......Golf es su juego.
Rodolfo.......Tiene dinero.
Rodolfo.......Conoce París.
Rodolfo.......¡Todo siempre le va muy bien!

Rodolfo va a París y ¡qué casualidad!
Mira a Julia Roberts y dice: "¡U la la!"
Entonces Rodolfito la invita a comer.
Julia lo acepta; no quiere ofender.

Estribillo nº 2:
Rodolfo.......Aventurero.
Rodolfo.......Va por crucero.
Rodolfo.......Tiene la suerte.
Rodolfo.......¡Todo siempre le va muy bien!

Pero ella paga todo. ¡Qué generosidad!
También le da un beso. ¡Qué casualidad!
Se sube al avión nuestro Rodolfito.
El avión se cae en el oceanito.

Estribillo nº 1

Todos están muertos excepto Rodolfito.
El crucero lo rescata; le regalan dinerito.
Y ya con tres millones tiene muchas opciones.
Va a Nueva York; compra tres habitaciones.

Estribillo nº 2

The song "Rodolfo" is based on the story "¡Qué casualidad!" in Chapter 1 of *¡Mírame, puedo hablar más!* by Blaine Ray and Joe Neilson.

♪♪¡Mírame, puedo cantar más!♪♪

Ejercicio nº 1

Rodolfo es un _____ , que _____ golf _____ bien.

Juega _____ Arnold Palmer y Jack Nicklaus _____ .

No juega por _____ , _____ centavitos.

Juega por _____ dólares por _____ hoyito.

Estribillo nº 1:

Rodolfo.......Golf _____ su juego.

Rodolfo......._____ dinero.

Rodolfo......._____ París.

_____ Todo siempre _____ _____ muy bien.

Rodolfo va a _____ y ¡ _____ _____ !

_____ ____ Julia Roberts y dice: "¡U la la!"

_____ Rodolfito _____ _____ a comer.

Julia _____ _____ ; no _____ ofender.

Estribillo nº 2:

Rodolfo......._____ .

Rodolfo.......Va por _____ .

Rodolfo......._____ la suerte.

Rodolfo.....¡Todo siempre _____ muy bien!

Pero ella _____ todo. ¡Qué _____!

_____ _____ _____ un beso. ¡Qué casualidad!

_____ _____ al avión _____ Rodolfito.

El _____ se cae en el _____ .

Estribillo nº 1

Todos están _____ _____ Rodolfito.

El crucero lo _____ ; _____ regalan dinerito.

Y ya con tres _____ tiene _____ opciones.

_____ _____ Nueva York; _____ tres habitaciones.

Estribillo nº 2

Ejercicio nº 2

Haz un círculo alrededor de la *c* o la *f*.   cierto   falso

1. Rodolfo es un hombre que juega béisbol.   c   f
2. Todo siempre le va muy mal.   c   f
3. Rodolfo viaja mucho.   c   f
4. Julia Roberts le da un beso a Rodolfo.   c   f
5. Rodolfo está muerto.   c   f

Ejercicio nº 3

Responde con frases completas.

6. Rodolfo juega golf por mil dólares o por centavitos por cada hoyito?

   _____

7. ¿Rodolfo conoce París o Madrid?

   _____

8. ¿Rodolfo le invita a Julia Roberts o a Christie Brinkley a comer?

9. ¿Rodolfo se sube a un avión o a un coche?

10. ¿Rodolfo dice: "¡Ay ay ay!" o "¡U la la!"?

Ejercicio nº 4

11. ¿Por qué juega golf Rodolfo?

12. ¿Por qué juega por tanto dinero Rodolfo?

13. ¿Por qué invita Rodolfo a Julia Roberts a comer?

14. ¿Por qué acepta Julia Roberts?

15. ¿Por qué se cae en el océano el avión de Rodolfo?

16. ¿Por qué siempre le va muy bien todo a Rodolfo?

17. ¿Cómo es que Rodolfo se encuentra en un crucero?

18. ¿Por qué es Rodolfo el único que vive cuando el avión se cae en el océano?

19. ¿Por qué le da un beso Julia a Rodolfo?

20. ¿Para qué necesita tres habitaciones Rodolfo?

Ejercicio nº 5

Haz seis dibujos que representan el cuento de Rodolfo y cuéntaselo a tu compañero(a) de clase.

1	2
3	4
5	6

♪♪¡*Mírame, puedo cantar más!* ♪♪

Vocabulario para "Nacha"

siempre	always
trata de	tries to
hacerse	(to) become
se alejan	they go away
la maltratan	they treat her badly, mistreat her
la dejan	they leave her
nunca	never
deja de	stops
apestar	to stink (stinking)
el jabón	the soap
francés	French
el maquillaje	the make-up
que se duche	let her take a shower (she needs to take a shower)
el champú	the shampoo
manzana	apple
se pone en la onda	gets "in the groove," gets "with it"
empiezan a	they begin to
mirar	to look at
tiene ganas de	wants to, feels like, has the desire to
bailar	to dance
besar	to kiss
lenta	slow
así que	so, therefore
se da cuenta	realizes
tiene que	has to
se tiene que bañar	has to take a bath
¿Qué te pasa?	What is the matter with you?
*mientras viéndola llorar	while seeing her cry
consejos	advice
le presta	loans him or her
†pa' que	so that
†pa' que vaya	so that she can go
tienda	store
comprar	to buy
la persiguen	they persue her
la molestan	they bother her
la siguen	they follow her
ya	now, already
se hizo	became

* The structure *mientras* _____ *-ndo* is used here in a poetic context; normally it is not correct grammar; the correct form is *mientras la ve llorando*.
† *Pa'* is a slang abbreviation of *para*.

Nacha

Nacha, pobre Nacha,
siempre trata de hacerse popular.
Los muchachos se alejan,
la maltratan y la dejan
porque ella nunca deja de apestar.
¿Qué necesita?

Estribillo:
Jabón inglés, perfume francés,
maquillaje italiano y jeans americanos;
que se duche en la mañana
con champú de la manzana.
Así se pone en la onda
y los muchachos la empiezan a mirar.

Nacha, pobre Nacha,
tiene ganas de bailar y de besar.
Pero ella es muy lenta,
así que nunca se da cuenta
de que uno sí se tiene que bañar.
¿Qué necesita?

Estribillo

"Nacha, ¿qué te pasa?"
dice Rosi mientras viéndola llorar*.
Y le da muchos consejos
y le presta unos pesos
pa' que vaya a la tienda a comprar.
¿Qué compra Nacha?

Estribillo

Nacha, feliz Nacha,
ahora no se tiene que preocupar.
Los muchachos la persiguen,
la molestan y la siguen.
¡Feliz Nacha ya se hizo popular!
¿Por qué?

Estribillo

---

* Please see note at the bottom of p. 18.

The song "Nacha" is based on the story "La chica social" in Chapter 2 of ¡*Mírame, puedo hablar más!* by Blaine Ray and Joe Neilson.

♪♪¡Mírame, puedo cantar más!♪♪

Ejercicio nº 1

Nacha, pobre Nacha,

siempre _____ _____ hacerse popular.

Los muchachos _____ _____ ,

la maltratan y la dejan

porque ella nunca _____ _____ apestar.

¿Qué necesita?

Estribillo:
Jabón inglés, _____ francés,

_____ _____ y jeans americanos;

que se duche en la _____

con _____ de la _____ .

_____ se pone en la onda

y los muchachos la _____ a mirar.

Nacha , pobre Nacha,

_____ _____ de bailar y de besar.

Pero ella es muy _____ ,

así que nunca _____ _____ _____

de que uno _____ se tiene que _____ .

¿Qué necesita?

Estribillo

♪♩¡Mírame, puedo cantar más!♪♩

"Nacha, ¿qué te pasa?" dice Rosi _____ viéndola llorar.

Y le da muchos _____

y _____ _____ unos pesos

pa' que vaya a la tienda a _____ .

¿Qué _____ Nacha?

Estribillo

Nacha, feliz Nacha,

_____ no se tiene que _____ .

Los muchachos _____ _____ ,

la _____ y la siguen.

¡Feliz Nacha ya _____ _____ _____ popular!

¿Por qué?

Estribillo

Ejercicio nº 2

Haz un círculo alrededor de la *c* o la *f*.

	cierto	falso
1. Nacha siempre trata de hacerse popular.	c	f
2. Los muchachos se acercan a Nacha.	c	f
3. Nacha nunca deja de apestar.	c	f
4. Nacha necesita perfume francés.	c	f
5. Nacha nota que Rosi está llorando.	c	f

♪♪ ¡Mírame, puedo cantar más! ♪♪

Ejercicio nº 3

Responde con frases completas.

6. ¿Nacha necesita jabón inglés o jabón Zest?

7. ¿Al fin los muchachos la empiezan a mirar o la empiezan a pegar?

8. ¿Nacha tiene ganas de apestar o de besar?

9. ¿Nacha es muy lenta o muy inteligente?

10. ¿Nacha no se da cuenta de que necesita bañarse o de que necesita vestirse?

Ejercicio nº 4

11. ¿Por qué necesita jeans americanos?

12. ¿Por qué llora Nacha?

13. ¿Qué va a comprar Nacha con el dinero que le dio Rosi?

14. Al fin de la canción, ¿por qué siguen y persiguen los muchachos a Nacha?

15. Al fin de la canción, ¿por qué está feliz Nacha?

♪♪¡Mírame, puedo cantar más!♪♪

16. ¿Por qué quiere ser popular Nacha?

17. ¿Por qué sabe Rosi cómo ser popular?

18. ¿Por qué es mejor el jabón inglés que el jabón japonés?

19. ¿Por qué tiene ganas de bailar y de besar Nacha?

20. ¿Por qué le da Rosi consejos a Nacha?

♪♪¡Mírame, puedo cantar más!♪♪

Ejercicio nº 5

Haz seis dibujos que relatan el cuento de Nacha en los rectángulos de abajo y cuéntale el cuento de Nacha a tu pareja. Los dibujos te ayudarán a recordar el cuento.

1	2
3	4
5	6

Vocabulario para "El café barato"

nos sentamos	we sit down
compramos	we buy
moscas	flies
el pan	the bread
muertas	dead
toscas	tough
bien cruda	very raw
se nos da	is given to us
con afán	with eagerness
todavía	still
me quiere	loves me
largo	long
grueso	thick
con aplomo	tactfully
el pastel	the cake
sucio	dirty
huele	smells
no aguanto	I can't stand it
se desmaya	faints
salgo	I leave
desesperado	in despair
mesero	waiter
ratero	thief
me la robó	stole her from me
casi	almost
es increíble	it's incredible
ya se olvidó	already forgot

El café barato

Caminando en la calle
con mi muchacha.
Nos sentamos en Mukdanals
y compramos hamburguesas.

Larvas de moscas en el pan,
muertas y toscas sí están.
Carne bien cruda se nos da.
Yo me la como con afán.
Ella todavía me quiere a mí.

Hay un pelo largo y grueso
en mi comida.
Yo la como con aplomo
para no ofenderla ya.

Estribillo:
En el pastel hay un calcetín
sucio que huele como Rin Tin Tin.
Yo no aguanto y vomito.
Se desmaya mi novia y yo no pago.
Ahora ella no me quiere a mí.

Yo me salgo enfadado,
desesperado.
Mi muchacha, pobre Nacha,
ya se desmayó.

Larvas de moscas en el pan,
muertas y toscas sí están.
Carne bien cruda se nos da*.
Yo me la como con afán.
Ahora ella no me quiere a mí.

El mesero es un ratero.
Él me la robó.
Casi imposible, es increíble
que de mí ya se olvidó.

Estribillo

* Some cassettes and CDs say "se nos dan," which is incorrect.

The song "El café barato" is based on the story "El restaurante elegante" in Chapter 3 of *¡Mírame, puedo hablar más!* by Blaine Ray and Joe Neilson.

♪♪¡Mírame, puedo cantar más!♪♪

Ejercicio nº 1

Caminando en la _____

con mi muchacha.

_____ _____ en Mukdanals

y compramos hamburguesas.

Larvas de _____ en el pan,

_____ y toscas sí están.

Carne bien cruda _____ _____ _____ .

_____ me la como con _____ .

Ella _____ me quiere a mí.

Hay un _____ largo y _____

en mi _____ .

Yo _____ _____ con aplomo

para no ofenderla ya.

Estribillo:

En el _____ hay un _____

sucio que _____ como Rin Tin Tin.

Yo no _____ y vomito.

_____ _____ mi _____ y yo no _____ .

Ahora ella no me _____ a mí.

♪♪¡Mírame, puedo cantar más!♪♪

Yo me _____ enfadado,

_____ .

Mi muchacha, pobre Nacha,

ya se _____ .

Larvas de _____ en el pan,

muertas y toscas sí _____ .

_____ bien cruda se nos da.

Yo _____ _____ _____ con afán.

Ahora ella no me _____ a mí.

El _____ es un ratero.

Él me la _____ .

Casi _____ , es increíble

que de mí ya _____ _____ .

Estribillo

Ejercicio nº 2

Haz un círculo alrededor de la **c** o la **f**.

	cierto	falso
1. Un muchacho y una muchacha están caminando en la casa.	c	f
2. Los muchachos se sientan en el restaurant Taco Flaco.	c	f
3. En el pan hay larvas de moscas.	c	f
4. El muchacho come carne bien cruda.	c	f
5. En el pastel hay dos perros sucios.	c	f

Ejercicio nº 3

Responde con frases completas.

6. ¿En el pastel hay un pie o un calcetín sucio?

7. ¿El muchacho vomita o se desmaya cuando encuentra el calcetín sucio?

8. ¿La novia se duerme o se desmaya?

9. ¿El muchacho paga o no paga?

Ejercicio nº 4

10. ¿Por qué es un ratero el mesero?

11. ¿Por qué se desmaya Nacha?

12. Nacha se olvidó de su novio. ¿Por qué es casi imposible?

13. ¿Por qué no quiere Nacha a su novio ahora?

14. ¿Por qué come el muchacho la carne con afán?

15. ¿Por qué piensa el muchacho que la muchacha no le quiere a él?

16. ¿Cómo come el muchacho el pelo grueso?

17. ¿Por qué compra hamburguesas el muchacho para Nacha?

18. ¿Por qué no aguanta el muchacho?

19. ¿Por qué huele como Rin Tin Tin el calcetín?

20. ¿Por qué es ridícula esta canción?

Ejercicio nº 5

Dibuja el cuento del café barato usando los seis marcos siguientes. Dibuja una escena diferente en cada marco. Después cuéntale el cuento a un(a) compañero(a) de clase.

1	2
3	4
5	6

♪♪ ¡Mírame, puedo cantar más! ♪♪

Vocabulario para "El restaurante elegante"

quiero	I want
la mujer	the woman
el ambiente	the atmosphere
mal	bad
mejor	better yet
la llevo	I'll take her
nos vamos	we go
sin vacilar	without hesitating
entramos	we enter
pedimos	we ask for, order
se despierta	wakes up
el pastel de fresas	the strawberry cake
a montón	by the pile
Esto, ¿qué es?	What is this?
no tengo ganas	I don't feel like
un calcetín sucio	a dirty sock
pelos de ratas	rat hairs
larvas de moscas	fly larvae (maggots)
comí	I ate
por fin	finally
llega	arrives
el afán	the eagerness
sabrosa	delicious, savory
el alacrán	the scorpion
mareada	dizzy, nauseous
se cae	falls down
desmayada	unconscious
me pregunto	I wonder
no lo puedo entender	I can't understand it
me pongo enojado	I become angry
bien preocupado	very worried
al ver	upon seeing
qué cuenta	what a bill
me la niego a pagar	I refuse to pay it
el mesero	the waiter
gigante	gigantic
se enamoran	they fall in love
no demoran	they don't hesitate
se casan	they get married
el balcón	the balcony
yo no más lloro	I just cry
el rincón	the corner
medio alerta	half alert
salgo enfadado	I leave angry
no la pago	I don't pay it
cuenta	bill, check

El restaurante elegante

Quiero pedir la mano
de la mujer que amo
pero el ambiente está mal.
Mejor la llevo a un restaurán.

A un restaurán nos vamos.
Sin vacilar entramos.
Pedimos filet mignón,
pastel de fresas a montón.

Estribillo:
"Esto, ¿qué es?" dijo mi
  comprometida.
De comer, yo no tengo ganas ya.
Un calcetín sucio,
pelos de ratas y larvas de moscas
  ya comí yo.

Por fin llega la sopa.
Es rica y deliciosa.
Como con mucho afán
sabrosa sopa de alacrán.

Se siente mareada.
Se cae; está desmayada.
Yo me pregunto ¿por qué?
Yo no lo puedo entender.

Estribillo

Me pongo enojado,
bien preocupado
al ver qué cuenta me dan.
Yo me la niego a pagar.

Yo salgo enfadado.
La cuenta no la pago.
Me subo al coche y me voy.
Pero con Nacha no estoy.

Estribillo

Mi novia se despierta.
Está medio alerta
en brazos del mesero.
Le da un gigante beso.

Los dos se enamoran.
Luego no demoran;
se casan en el balcón.
Yo no más lloro en el rincón.

Estribillo

The song "El restaurante elegante" is based on the story of the same name in Chapter 3 of *¡Mírame, puedo hablar más!* by Blaine Ray and Joe Neilson.

♪♪¡Mírame, puedo cantar más!♪♪

Ejercicio nº 1

Quiero _____ la mano

de la _____ que amo

pero el _____ está mal.

Mejor _____ _____ a un restaurán.

A _____ restaurán nos vamos.

_____ vacilar entramos.

_____ filet miñón,

_____ _____ _____ a montón.

Estribillo:

"Esto, ¿qué es?" dijo mi _____ .

De comer, yo no _____ _____ ya.

Un calcetín _____ ,

pelos de _____ y larvas de _____ ya comí yo.

Por fin _____ la sopa.

Es _____ y deliciosa.

Como con mucho _____

_____ sopa de alacrán.

Se siente _____ .

Se cae; está _____ .

34

♪♫¡Mírame, puedo cantar más!♫♪

_____ me pregunto ¿_____ _____?

_____ no lo _____ entender.

Estribillo

_____ _____ enojado,

bien _____

_____ ver qué _____ me dan.

Yo me la niego a _____ .

Yo salgo _____ .

_____ cuenta no la pago.

_____ _____ al coche y me voy.

Pero con Nacha no _____ .

Estribillo

Mi novia se _____ .

Está _____ alerta

en _____ del mesero.

Le da un gigante _____ .

Los dos se _____ .

Luego no _____ ;

_____ _____ en el _____ .

Yo no más _____ en el rincón.

♪♪¡Mírame, puedo cantar más!♪♪

Estribillo
Ejercicio nº 2

Haz un círculo alrededor de la *c* o la *f*.   cierto   falso

1. Un muchacho quiere pedir la mano de una muchacha.   c   f

2. El muchacho decide llevarle a la muchacha al cine.   c   f

3. La muchacha pide muchas palomitas en el cine.   c   f

4. Van a un restaurante y piden filet mignón.   c   f

5. La muchacha encuentra cosas sucias en la comida.   c   f

Ejercicio nº 3

Responde con frases completas.

6. En el pastel, ¿la muchacha encuentra un calcetín sucio o una culebra?
   _____

7. ¿La muchacha come pelos de rata o cabeza de vaca?
   _____

8. ¿La sopa es deliciosa o no es deliciosa?
   _____

9. ¿El muchacho come la sopa con mucho afán o con cuidado?
   _____

10. ¿La sopa es de mosquitos o de alacrán?
    _____

Ejercicio nº 4

La información en las siguientes frases está incorrecta. Escríbelas de nuevo con la información correcta.

11. El muchacho paga la cuenta porque la comida está muy buena. El está muy feliz.

   _____

12. La novia del muchacho se llama Catalina.

   _____

13. La novia se despierta en los brazos de su novio.

   _____

14. Hay un pastel dentro de un calcetín limpio.

   _____

15. La muchacha tiene muchas ganas de comer.

   _____

Ejercicio nº 5

Responde a las preguntas.

16. ¿Por qué se sube al coche y se va el muchacho?

   _____

17. ¿Quién le da un gigante beso a quién?

   _____

18. ¿Por qué se enamoran el mesero y Nacha?

   _____

19. ¿Dónde se casan el mesero y Nacha?

   _____

20. ¿Por qué llora en el rincón el muchacho?

   _____

♪♪¡Mírame, puedo cantar más!♪♪

Ejercicio nº 6

Dibuja el cuento del restaurante elegante en los seis rectángulos que siguen. Entonces cuéntale el cuento a tu pareja.

1	2
3	4
5	6

Vocabulario para "Los perros olímpicos"

tienen ganas de	have the desire to, want to
ganar	to win
siempre	always
nunca	never
te distraerán	will distract you
dejan de	stop, cease
viejas	girls (slang; actually means "old women")
tratando de	trying to
moviendo sus colitas	moving their tails
con fin de	with the goal of
las resisten	they resist them
insisten	they insist
hueso	bone
oro	gold
se gana	is earned, is won
fueron	they were
exitosas	successful
logrando	succeeding in
sin las motas	without the spots
festejando	"partying," celebrating
tomando	drinking
bailando	dancing
les ofrecen	offer them
no le interesa	doesn't interest him
cada día	every day
cayó en las tentaciones	fell into the temptation
no pudo	he could not
resistirlas	resist them
negar	deny
ni	nor
evadirlas	escape them, evade them
moraleja	moral
diré	I will say
sigue	continue
lograrás	you will succeed in, you will achieve
vicios	vices

♪♪ ¡*Mírame, puedo cantar más!* ♪♪

Los perros olímpicos

Los perros olímpicos
tienen ganas de ganar.
Los perros olímpicos
nunca dejan de entrenar.

Ya vienen dos perritas,
tratando de atraerles,
moviendo sus colitas
con fin de distraerles.
Los perros las resisten
porque ellos insisten
que el hueso de oro no se gana así.

Estribillo:
Los perros olímpicos, ¡ay ay ay!
Los perros olímpicos, ¡ay ay ay!
Los perros olímpicos, ¡ay ay ay!,
nunca dejan de entrenar.

Pues, fueron exitosas
las dos perras hermosas.
Logrando distraerle*
al perro sin las motas.
Andan festejando,
tomando y bailando.
El hueso de oro no se gana así.

Los perros olímpicos, ¡ay ay ay!
Los perros olímpicos, ¡ay ay ay!
Los perros olímpicos, ¡ay ay ay!,
tienen ganas de ganar.

Las perras les ofrecen
cigarrillos y cerveza
pero al perrito fuerte
no le interesan.
Corre cada día
veinticinco millas.
El hueso de oro no se gana así.

Estribillo

El perro con las motas
ahora triste está.
Cayó en las tentaciones
de las muchachitas.
No pudo resistirlas,
negar ni evadirlas†.
El hueso de oro no se gana así.

El perro olímpico, ¡ay ay ay!
El perro olímpico, ¡ay ay ay!
El perro olímpico, ¡ay ay ay!,
gana todo el maratón.

Oye la moreleja;
te la diré a ti.
Sigue con tus metas
y lograrás tu fin.
Los vicios y las viejas
siempre te distraerán.
El hueso de oro no se gana así.

El perro flojísimo, ¡ay ay ay!
El perro flojísimo, ¡ay ay ay!
El perro flojísimo, ¡ay ay ay!,
ni un hueso frito alcanzó.

Estribillo

---

* Some cassettes and CDs say "logrando en distraerle," which is incorrect.
† Some cassettes and CDs say "negar o evadirlas," which is incorrect.

The song "Los perros olímpicos" is based on the story of the same name in Chapter 4 of *¡Mírame, puedo hablar más!* by Blaine Ray and Joe Neilson.

♪♪¡Mírame, puedo cantar más!♪♪

Ejercicio nº 1

Los _____ olímpicos

_____ _____ de ganar.

Los perros _____

_____ dejan de entrenar.

____ vienen dos perritas,

_____ ____ atraerles,

_____ sus colitas

_____ _____ ___ distraerles.

Los perros _____ resisten

porque ellos _____

que el _____ ____

_____ no se gana así.

Estribillo:

Los perros _____, ¡ay ay ay!

Los perros olímpicos, ¡ _____

____ ____ !

____ _____

_____ , ¡ay ay ay!,

_____ dejan de entrenar.

_____ , fueron exitosas

_____ _____ perras hermosas.

Logrando _____

al perro _____ las motas.

Andan _____ ,

_____ y bailando.

El hueso de oro _____ _____

_____ _____ .

Los perros _____, ¡ay ay ay!

Los _____ olímpicos, ¡ay ay ay!

Los perros olímpicos, ¡ _____

_____ _____ !,

tienen ganas de _____ .

41

♪♪¡Mírame, puedo cantar más!♪♪

Las perras _____

_____

cigarrillos y _____

pero ___ perrito fuerte

no le _____ .

Corre _____ día

_____ millas.

El _____ de oro no se gana así.

Estribillo

El perro con las _____

ahora _____ está.

_____ en las tentaciones

de las _____ .

No _____ resistirlas,

_____ ni evadirlas.

El hueso de _____ no se gana así.

El perro _____ , ¡ay ay ay!

El _____ olímpico, ¡ay ay ay!

El perro olímpico, ¡ _____ _____ _____ !,

gana todo el _____ .

Oye la _____ ;

____ ____ diré a ti.

_____ con tus metas

y _____ tu fin.

Los _____ y las viejas

_____ te distraerán.

El hueso de oro no _____

_____ así.

El perro _____ , ¡ay ay ay!

El perro flojísimo, ¡ _____ _____ _____ !

____ _____ flojísimo, ¡ay ay ay!,

ni un hueso _____ alcanzó.

Estribillo

Ejercicio nº 2

Haz un círculo alrededor de la *c* o la *f*.   cierto   falso

1. Los perros olímpicos tienen ganas de besar.   c   f

2. Dos perritas también se entrenan para los juegos olímpicos.   c   f

3. Las dos perras mueven sus piernas para distraer a los perros.   c   f

4. Los perros deciden no entrenarse y siguen a las perritas.   c   f

5. Sólo el perro con las motas se entrena.   c   f

Ejercicio nº 3

Responde con frases completas.

6. ¿El perro con las motas anda festejando o ladrando?

   _____

7. ¿El hueso de oro se gana o no se gana festejando, tomando y bailando?

   _____

8. ¿Las perras les ofrecen cigarrillos o Coca-Cola?

   _____

9. ¿Al perrito fuerte no le interesa o sí le interesa la cerveza?

   _____

10. ¿El perro olímpico corre veintitrés millas cada día o veinticinco millas?

    _____

♪♪ ¡Mírame, puedo cantar más! ♪♪

Ejercicio nº 4

11. ¿Por qué está tan triste el perro con las motas?

12. ¿Cuántos perros en total hay en esta canción?

13. ¿Por qué no se cayó en las tentaciones de las perritas el perro sin las motas?

14. ¿Por qué no pudo resistir, negar ni evadir las perras el perro con las motas?

15. ¿Cómo se gana el hueso de oro?

16. ¿Por qué pierde el maratón el perro flojo?

17. ¿Por qué gana todo el maratón el perro sin las motas?

18. ¿Cuál es la moraleja de la canción?

19. ¿Por qué quieren distraer a los perros las perras?

20. ¿Por qué logran distraer las perras al perro con las motas y no al perro sin las motas?

♪♪¡Mírame, puedo cantar más!♪♪

Ejercicio nº 5

Dibuja el cuento de los perros olímpicos en seis escenas. Usa los marcos siguientes — un marco para cada escena. Después cuéntale oralmente el cuento "Los perros olímpicos" a tu pareja.

1	2
3	4
5	6

♪♪¡Mírame, puedo cantar más!♪♪

Vocabulario para "El carro de mi familia"

puedo olvidar	I can forget
porque	because
nunca	never
le faltaba	was lacking (on it)
algo	something
nunca le faltaba algo que reparar	it never failed to have something that needed to be repaired
¿Me prestas?	Will you lend me?
solía	I used to
lo siento	I'm sorry
hijo de mi vida	my dear son (son of my life)
el taller	the shop
se le rompió el parabrisas	the windshield broke on it
los frenos	the brakes
no están	are gone
llanta	tire
no dan luz	don't shine (don't give light)
gastado	worn out
la bobina	the coil
quemada	burnt
a lo mejor	probably
deberías	you should
el anticogelante	the antifreeze
chorreando	leaking
tratas de arrancarlo	you try to start it
el rencor	the anger
por todos lados	everywhere
petardeando	backfiring
me da pena	it troubles me, makes me sad (gives me sorrow)
lata	can
basura	rubbish
se le cayó	fell off of it
el parachoques	the bumper
pintura	paint
se rayó	got scratched
rumbo a	on the way to
librería	bookstore
grúa	tow truck
se chocó con	crashed into
el capó	the hood
se fue volando	went flying
se le ocurrió	it occurred to her
echarle gasolina	to throw gasoline on it
cerrillo	match
lo prendió	lit it
oye tú	listen
la moraleja	the moral
preocupada	worried
si te falta un transporte	if you are lacking a vehicle, transportation
te digo	I tell you
de verdad	truly
cómprate una bicicleta	buy yourself a bicycle

El carro de mi familia

Estribillo:
El carro de mi familia no lo puedo olvidar
porque nunca le faltaba algo que reparar.
"¿Me prestas las llaves?, Papi", solía yo preguntar.
"Lo siento, hijo de mi vida, porque en el taller está."

"Se le rompió el parabrisas y los frenos no están.
Una llanta está pinchada y las luces luz no dan.
El coche está gastado. La bobina quemada está.
A lo mejor, hijo mío, deberías caminar."

Estribillo

"El anticogelante está chorreando del motor.
Cuando tratas de arrancarlo, te responde con rencor.
Vibrando por todos lados, petardeando pa' aquí y allá,
me da pena, hijo mío, esa lata de basura."

Se le cayó el parachoques; la pintura se rayó.
Rumbo a la librería con una grúa se chocó.
Cuando el capó se fue volando, a Mamá se le ocurrió
echarle gasolina y con cerillo lo prendió.

Estribillo

Oye tú la moraleja y tu vida estará
menos complicada y preocupada.
Si te falta un transporte, te digo de verdad:
cómprate una bicicleta; tus problemas se irán.

Estribillo

The song "El carro de mi familia" is based on the story "El carro de la familia" in Chapter 5 of ¡*Mírame, puedo hablar más!* by Blaine Ray and Joe Neilson.

♪♪¡Mírame, puedo cantar más!♪♪

Ejercicio nº 1

Estribillo:

El carro de mi familia no lo _____ olvidar

porque nunca _____ _____ algo que reparar.

"¿_____ prestas las llaves, Papi?", _____ yo preguntar.

"Lo siento, hijo de mi vida, porque en el _____ está."

"Se le rompió el _____ y los frenos no están.

Una _____ está _____ y las luces luz no dan.

El coche está gastado. La bobina _____ está.

____ _____ _____ , hijo mío, deberías caminar."

Estribillo:

El _____ de mi familia no lo puedo _____ .

_____ _____ le faltaba algo que reparar.

"¿_____ _____ las _____ Papi?", solía yo preguntar.

"_____ _____ , hijo de mi vida, porque en el taller está."

"El _____ está _____ del motor.

Cuando tratas de _____ , te responde con rencor.

Vibrando _____ _____ _____ , petardeando pa' aquí y

_____ ,

_____ _____ _____ , hijo mío, esa lata de _____ ."

♪♪¡Mírame, puedo cantar más!♪♪

_____ _____ _____ el _____ ; la

_____ se rayó.

Rumbo a la _____ con una _____ se chocó.

_____ el capó se fue volando, a Mamá _____ _____

_____

echarle gasolina y con cerillo lo _____ .

Estribillo

_____ tú la moraleja y tu _____ estará

menos complicada y _____ .

Si _____ _____ un _____ , te digo de verdad:

_____ una _____ ; tus _____
   se irán.

Estribillo

Ejercicio nº 2

Haz un círculo alrededor de la *c* o la *f*.   cierto   falso

  1. Esta canción se trata de una bicicleta.   c   f

  2. El carro de la familia está en el baño.   c   f

  3. El carro no tiene frenos.   c   f

  4. Al carro se le cayó el parabrisas.   c   f

  5. El carro nunca está arreglado.   c   f

♪♪¡Mírame, puedo cantar más!♪♪

Ejercicio nº 3

Responde con frases completas.

6. ¿Qué esta chorreando del motor — aceite, agua o anticogelante?

   _____

7. ¿Con qué se chocó el carro rumbo a la librería — con una grúa o con una casa?

   _____

8. ¿Qué hizo la mamá con un cerillo — prendió un cigarrillo o prendió la gasolina?

   _____

9. ¿Por qué no puede prestarle las llaves al muchacho el papá — porque el carro está en el taller o porque las llaves están perdidas?

   _____

10. ¿Qué está vibrando — la nave espacial del hijo o el carro de la familia?

    _____

Ejercicio nº 4

11. ¿Qué está chorreando del motor?

    _____

12. ¿Con qué se chocó el carro rumbo a la librería?

    _____

13. ¿Qué hizo la mamá con un cerillo?

    _____

14. ¿Por qué no puede prestarle las llaves al muchacho el papá?

    _____

15. ¿Qué está vibrando?

    _____

16. ¿Con qué prendió el carro?

17. ¿Qué le da pena al papá del muchacho?

18. ¿Qué debe comprar uno para no tener problemas?

19. ¿Qué parte del coche fue volando?

20. ¿Qué dice el papá que el hijo debería hacer?

21. ¿Cuál es el problema con la llanta?

22. ¿Cuándo responde con rencor el carro?

23. ¿Cuándo se le ocurrió a la mamá echarle gasolina al carro?

24. ¿Por qué no puede el muchacho olvidar el carro de la familia?

25. ¿Por qué va a la librería la mamá?

♪♪¡*Mírame, puedo cantar más!*♪♪

Ejercicio nº 5

Dibuja el cuento de la canción "El carro de mi familia" en seis escenas, usando los siguientes marcos. Entonces cuéntale el cuento a un compañero de clase.

1	2
3	4
5	6

Vocabulario para "Supermujer"

me dicen	they call me
esto	this
tengo que conceder	I have to concede
¿Cómo lo puede hacer?	How can she do it?
magia	magic
yo soy	I am
el poder	the power
le cuido	I take care of him
esta casa	this house
es su nido	is his nest
mientras que	while
tiendo la cama	I make the bed
me despierto	I wake up
me baño	I bathe
me afeito	I shave
me pongo	I put on
me rizo el pelo	I curl my hair
le canto	I sing to him
el amor de mis anhelos	the love of my desires (dreams)
entonces	then
me subo	I get in (a vehicle)
las mando	I send them
a través de	through, by means of
al llegar	upon arriving
luego	then
pongo la mesa	I set the table
ya es hora	it is now time
se levanta	gets out of, gets up

♪♪¡Mírame, puedo cantar más!♪♪

Supermujer

Estribillo:
Me dicen super super
　supermujer.
Esto sí tengo que conceder.
Las otras muchachas me miran
y dicen: "¿Cómo lo puede hacer?"
Pues, de magia no tiene nada que
　ver.
Yo soy la que tiene el poder.
A mi esposo yo le cuido.
Esta casa es su nido.

Me levanto en la mañana
y, mientras que estoy yo dormida,
tiendo la camita y preparo la
　comida.
Entonces me despierto y me baño
　y me afeito.
Y mientras que esto pasa,
lavo los platos de la casa.
Yo me pongo el maquillaje
y me rizo todo el pelo
y le canto a mi esposo,
el amor de mis anhelos.

Estribillo

Entonces me subo a mi Jaguar.
El coche me lleva a trabajar.
Escribo tres cartas con
　computadora.
y las mando através de mi
celular.
Al llegar a mi companía
yo trabajo todo el día.
Yo llamo al presidente
y me habla inmediatamente.

Estribillo

Al llegar a mi casita
yo preparo la comida.
Luego limpio las ventanas
y pongo la mesita.
Despierto a mi esposo.
Ya es hora de comer.
Se levanta de la cama
pa' comer y pa' beber.
Y luego él me dice:
"¡Buen trabajo!, mi querer."

Estribillo

The song "Supermujer" is based on the story "Los dos esposos" in Chapter 6 of ¡Mírame, puedo hablar más! by Blaine Ray and Joe Neilson.

♪♫¡Mírame, puedo cantar más!♫♪

Ejercicio nº 1

Estribillo:

Me _____ super super supermujer.

Esto sí _____ _____ conceder.

Las _____ muchachas _____ _____

y dicen: "¿ _____ lo puede hacer?"

Pues, de magia _____ _____ nada que ver.

Yo soy la que tiene _____ _____ .

A mi _____ yo le cuido.

_____ casa es su _____ .

_____ _____ en la mañana

y, _____ _____ estoy yo dormida,

_____ la camita y _____ la comida.

Entonces _____ _____ y me baño y _____ _____ .

Y _____ que esto _____ , lavo los platos de la casa.

Yo me pongo el _____

y _____ _____ todo el pelo

y _____ _____ a mi _____ ,

el amor de mis _____ .

Estribillo

♪♪¡Mírame, puedo cantar más!♪♪

Entonces _____ _____ a mi Jaguar.

El coche _____ _____ a trabajar.

_____ tres _____ con computadora.

y las mando _____ de mi celular.

_____ _____ a mi companía

yo _____ todo el día.

Yo llamo _____ presidente

y me habla _____ .

Estribillo

_____ _____ a mi casita

yo _____ la comida.

_____ limpio las _____

y _____ la mesita.

_____ a mi esposo.

Ya es _____ de comer.

_____ _____ de la cama

pa' comer y pa' _____ .

Y _____ él me dice:

"¡ _____ _____ !, mi querer."

♪♪¡Mírame, puedo cantar más!♪♪

♪♪¡Mírame, puedo cantar más!♪♪

Estribillo:

_____ _____ super super supermujer.

_____ sí tengo que _____ .

Las _____ muchachas _____ _____

y dicen: "¿Cómo _____ _____ _____ ?"

Pues de _____ no tiene nada que ver.

Yo _____ la que tiene el _____ .

A mi esposo yo _____ _____ .

_____ casa es su nido.

Ejercicio nº 2

Haz un círculo alrededor de la *c* o la *f*.   cierto   falso

1. Le dicen superperra a la mujer en la canción.   c   f

2. Las otras muchachas la miran y dicen: "Llámame por celular."   c   f

3. La mujer de la canción dice que ella es la que tiene el poder.   c   f

4. La mujer de la canción dice que su casa es el nido del esposo.   c   f

5. La mujer se despierta antes de preparar la comida.   c   f

Ejercicio nº 3

Responde con frases completas.

6. ¿La mujer de la canción se baña en la mañana o en la noche?

_____

7. Mientras que se baña y se afeita, ¿ella lava los platos o besa a su esposo?

_____

8. Cuando la mujer de la canción se pone el maquillaje y se riza el pelo, ¿ella canta o le grita a su esposo?

_____

9. ¿La mujer maneja un Chevrolet o un Jaguar?
   _____

10. ¿La mujer manda sus cartas através del correo o através de su celular?
    _____

Ejercicio nº 4

11. ¿Por qué trabaja todo el día la mujer?
    _____

12. ¿Para qué le llama al presidente por teléfono?
    _____

13. ¿Qué hace la mujer entre limpiar las ventanas y poner la mesita?
    _____

14. ¿Quién se levanta de la cama pa' comer y pa' beber?
    _____

15. ¿Por qué le habla inmediatamente el presidente a Supermujer?
    _____

16. ¿Qué dicen las otras mujeres cuando la miran?
    _____

17. ¿Por qué es la casa del hombre su nido?
    _____

18. ¿Qué hace Supermujer con su computadora en el coche?
    _____

19. ¿Por qué se riza todo el pelo y no una parte?
    _____

20. La mujer dice que la magia no tiene nada que ver con su poder. ¿Por qué dice eso?
    _____

Ejercicio nº 5

Haz seis dibujos que representan el cuento de Supermujer y cuéntaselo a tu compañero(a) de clase.

1	2
3	4
5	6

THE AUTHOR

Gale Mackey — teacher, workshop leader, and songwriter — has been teaching Spanish for 31 years (as of 2001) and utilizing songs as a vital part of his teaching repertoire. Gale currently teaches TPR Storytelling Spanish at Stockdale High School in Bakersfield, California, where he lives with his wife Kristen and their five children.

DISTRIBUTORS
of Command Performance Language Institute materials

Midwest European
  Publications
915 Foster St.
Evanston, IL 60201-3199
(847) 866-6289
(800) 380-8919
Fax (847) 866-6290
info@mep-eli.com
www.mep-eli.com

Miller Educational
  Materials
P.O. Box 2428
Buena Park, CA 90621
(800) MEM 4 ESL
Toll Free Fax (888) 462-0042
MillerEdu@aol.com
www.millereducational.com

Tempo Bookstore
4905 Wisconsin Ave., N.W.
Washington, DC 20016
(202) 363-6683
Fax (202) 363-6686
Tempobookstore@usa.net

Multi-Cultural Books
  & Videos
28880 Southfield Rd.,
  Suite 183
Lathrup Village, MI 48076
(248) 559-2676
(800) 567-2220
Fax (248) 559-2465
service@multiculbv.com
www.multiculbv.com

World of Reading, Ltd.
P.O. Box 13092
Atlanta, GA 30324-0092
(404) 233-4042
(800) 729-3703
Fax (404) 237-5511
polyglot@wor.com
www.wor.com

Educational Showcase
3519 E. Ten Mile Rd.
Warren, MI 48091
(810) 758-3013
(800) 213-3671
Fax (810) 756-2016

Carlex
P.O. Box 81786
Rochester, MI 48308-1786
(800) 526-3768
Fax (248) 852-7142
www.carlexonline.com

Berty Segal, Inc.
1749 E. Eucalyptus St.
Brea, CA 92821
(714) 529-5359
Fax (714) 529-3882
BertySegal@aol.com
www.tprsource.com

Entry Publishing
  & Consulting
P.O. Box 20277
New York, NY 10025
(212) 662-9703
Toll Free (888) 601-9860
Fax: (212) 662-0549

The English Resource
15-15-2F Matsugae-cho
Sagamihara-shi,
  Kanagawa-ken
JAPAN 228
Tel 042-744-8898
Fax 042-744-8897
resource@twics.com

Calliope Books
Route 3, Box 3395
Saylorsburg, PA 18353
Tel/Fax (610) 381-2587

BookLink
465 Broad Ave.
Leonia, NJ 07605
(201) 947-3471
Fax (201) 947-6321
booklink@intac.com

Edumate
2231 Morena Blvd.
San Diego, CA 92110
(619) 275-7117
Fax (619) 275-7120
GusBla@aol.com

Authors & Editors
10736 Jefferson Blvd. #104
Culver City, CA 90230
(310) 836-2014

Canadian Resources for
  ESL
15 Ravina Crescent
Toronto, Ontario
CANADA M4J 3L9
(416) 466-7875
Fax (416) 466-4383
Thane@interlog.com
www.interlog.com/~thane

Alta Book Center
14 Adrian Court
Burlingame, CA 94010
(650) 692-1285
(800) ALTAESL
Fax (650) 692-4654
Fax (800) ALTAFAX
info@altaesl.com
www.altaesl.com

European Book Co.
925 Larkin St.
San Francisco, CA 94109
(415) 474-0626

Delta Systems, Inc.
1400 Miller Parkway
McHenry, IL 60050
(815) 36-DELTA
(800) 323-8270
Fax (800) 909-9901
custsvc@delta-systems.com
www.delta-systems.com

International Book Centre
2391 Auburn Rd.
Shelby Township, MI 48317
(810) 879-8436
Fax (810) 254-7230

Athelstan
2476 Bolsover,
  Suite 464
Houston, TX 77005
(713) 523-2837
Fax (713) 523-6543
barlow@athel.com
www.athel.com

David English House
6F Seojung Bldg.
1308-14 Seocho 4 Dong
Seocho-dong
Seoul 137-074
KOREA
Tel 02)594-7625
Fax 02)591-7626
hkhwang1@chollian.net
www.eltkorea.com

Continental Book Co.
625 E. 70th Ave., Unit 5
Denver, CO 80229
(303) 289-1761
Fax (800) 279-1764
esl@continentalbook.com
www.continentalbook.com

Sky Oaks Productions
P.O. Box 1102
Los Gatos, CA 95031
(408) 395-7600
Fax (408) 395-8440
TPR World@aol.com
www.tpr-world.com

Multi-Cultural Books
  & Videos
12033 St. Thomas Crescent
Tecumseh, ONT
CANADA N8N 3V6
(519) 735-3313
Fax (519) 735-5043
service@multiculbv.com
www.multiculbv.com

Applause Learning
  Resources
85 Fernwood Lane
Roslyn, NY 11576-1431
(516) 365-1259
(800) APPLAUSE
Toll Free Fax
  (877) 365-7484
www.applauselearning.com

Sosnowski Language
  Resources
58 Sears Rd.
Wayland, MA 01778
(508) 358-7891
Fax (508) 358-6687
sosnow@ma.ultranet.com

Teacher's Discovery
2741 Paldan Dr.
Auburn Hills, MI 48326
(800) TEACHER
(248) 340-7210
Fax (248) 340-7212
www.teachersdiscovery.com

Continental Book Co.
80-00 Cooper Ave. #29
Glendale, NY 11385
(718) 326-0560
Fax (718) 326-4276
www.continentalbook.com

SpeakWare
2836 Stephen Dr.
Richmond, CA 94803
(510) 222-2455
leds@speakware.com
www.speakware.com